DISPOSAL OF WEST SIDE RAILROAD TRACKS

A REPORT TO THE MERCHANTS' ASSOCIATION OF NEW YORK BY ITS COMMITTEE ON DISPOSAL OF WEST SIDE RAILROAD TRACKS

NOVEMBER 25, 1908

THE MERCHANTS' ASSOCIATION OF NEW YORK

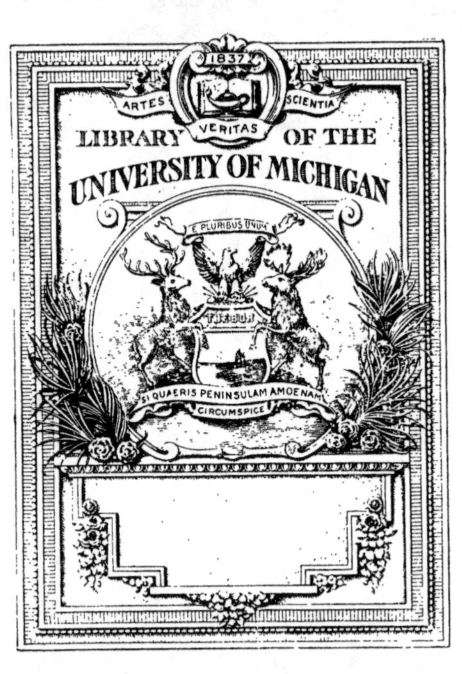

DISPOSAL OF WEST SIDE RAILROAD TRACKS

A REPORT TO THE MERCHANTS' ASSOCIATION OF NEW YORK BY ITS COMMITTEE ON DISPOSAL OF WEST SIDE RAILROAD TRACKS

NOVEMBER 25, 1908

THE MERCHANTS' ASSOCIATION OF NEW YORK

THE
MERCHANTS' ASSOCIATION OF NEW YORK

OFFICERS

DIRECTORS

COMMITTEE
ON DISPOSAL OF WEST SIDE R. R. TRACKS

WALTER C. KERR, *Chairman*
JOHN M. CARRERE
W. J. MATHESON
E. H. OUTERBRIDGE
GEORGE C. SMITH

PREFATORY.

THE Legislature of 1906 enacted a law (Chapter 109, Laws of 1906) requiring the removal of the railroad tracks of the New York Central & Hudson River Railroad Company from the surface of Tenth and Eleventh Avenues, West, Canal, Hudson and all other streets in the Borough of Manhattan. It provided that the tracks so removed from the surface might be placed in a subway beneath those or other streets, to be constructed at the expense of the Company, if a route and plan for such subway should be agreed upon within one year by the Rapid Transit Commission and the Company. In default of such agreement, it was made the duty of the Rapid Transit Commission (since succeeded by the Public Service Commission) to begin proceedings for the condemnation of the franchise rights and property of the Company in the streets now occupied by it.

It was the judgment of the Rapid Transit Commission that the construction of a freight subway as required by the law is open to many objections of the most serious nature, and therefore undesirable. The difficulties of construction would be very great, the obstacles in the way of proper operation practically insuperable, and the cost commercially prohibitive. For these reasons the Railroad Company refused to undertake the construction of the proposed freight subway.

No agreement having been reached within the time prescribed, the Public Service Commission, as required by the terms of the law, began condemnation proceedings, preliminary to the removal of the tracks, which proceedings are now in progress.

The removal of the existing tracks and terminal stations without the provision of equal alternative facilities would impose a very heavy burden of additional cost upon shippers. An adequate freight terminal for the N. Y. C. & H. R. R. upon the water front, served by lighters, cannot be secured. A large portion of shipments would, therefore, of necessity require to be carted at excessive cost from the lower part of the City to the 60th Street terminal.

It is, therefore, of the first importance to the City's business interests that an effective alternative plan be devised, which shall provide for the removal of the tracks from the surface of the streets, preserve or increase existing facilities, and avoid the objections which make a subway impracticable.

The Public Service Commission, although restricted by the Saxe Act to either a subway or the entire removal of the tracks, has power to prepare other plans and recommend to the Legislature legislation necessary to make them effective. The Association's Committee on Removal of West Side Tracks was appointed for the purpose of studying the problem created by the Legislative action above referred to, with a view to finding a practicable alternative, and presenting it for the consideration of the Public Service Commission. The following Report is directed to that end.

ACTION BY THE BOARD OF DIRECTORS UPON REPORT OF THE COMMITTEE ON DISPOSAL OF WEST SIDE RAILROAD TRACKS.

AT a special meeting of the Board of Directors of The Merchants' Association of New York, called November 25, 1908, to consider a Report of the Committee on Disposal of West Side Railroad Tracks, which report is printed herewith, the folowing preambles and resolution were adopted:

WHEREAS, The able Special Committee appointed by The Merchants' Association of New York to investigate and report on the subject of the *Disposal of West Side Railroad Tracks,* after more than a year's study of the subject, has embodied its conclusions and recommendations in the report presented to the Board of Directors at its meeting held November 13, 1908, the Executive Committee having previously given the report careful consideration and recommended its adoption, and

WHEREAS, The Board, at said meeting, after listening to the reading of the report *in extenso,* ordered that copies be made for each member, and deferred action thereon until a special adjourned meeting, two weeks later, in order that in the interim each member of the Board might have opportunity carefully to study the report, and

WHEREAS, Said report thus having been most carefully considered by the Special Committee, by the Executive Committee, and by this Board; now, therefore,

RESOLVED, That the report is hereby accepted by the Board of Directors of The Merchants' Association of New York, as covering a definite and practical plan for the solution of the problem to which the report relates, and that the report be duly presented to the Public Service Commission of the First District.

That in submitting this report to said Commission, in response to its suggestion, as a contribution by The Merchants' Association to the solution of the problems involved, attention is called to the definite and practical character of the plan presented; to the progressive steps by which the plan can be inaugurated and carried forward, each step being comparatively independent, yet mutually interdependent when all are completed; and to the many subordinate but related problems which will be solved by the adoption and carrying out of the complete plan.

That the Public Service Commission be requested to authorize its engineering and other departments to perfect a plan embodying such of the recommendations in said report as may be found feasible and advantageous to the end that a definite, comprehensive, and practical plan may be developed for the solution of the problems involved, worked out with sufficient detail to enable reliable estimates of cost to be made, and also to enable the public to form an intelligent opinion concerning the merits of the plan as contrasted with others which may be proposed, and the expediency of adopting it.

S. C. MEAD, *Secretary.*

DISPOSAL OF WEST SIDE RAILROAD TRACKS.

NEW YORK, November 5, 1908.

To the Board of Directors of The Merchants' Association of New York:

GENTLEMEN:

YOUR Committee, appointed November 18, 1907, upon the matter commonly known as the West Side Transportation Problem has the honor to make the following report:

SUBJECTS EMBRACED.

1. The desirability of freight tracks on or above West Street and its Marginal Way, some five miles long and 250 feet wide, between the east line of West Street and the Hudson River bulkhead line.
2. The construction of warehouses in connection therewith.
3. The removal or the readjustment of the surface tracks of the N. Y. C. & H. R. R. Co. now on or near the Hudson River Water front and in Tenth and Eleventh Avenues.
4. Other considerations which may be relevant to the whole problem, such as passenger transportation.

GENERAL REMARKS.

YOUR Committee believe that it is practically impossible to devise a plan sufficiently covering all future necessities, but it is believed that measures can be adopted which will result in benefit now, much more in the near future, and be sufficiently consistent with municipal evolution to enable the proper authorities from time to time to so construct as to meet the growing needs when and as they develop.

The Committee has reviewed the work of prior committees, commissions, engineers, and reports of committees of public bodies on matters relating directly and indirectly to the several divisions of this subject. It has inspected all of the area under consideration and has made a study of the physical conditions, character of territory, and the traffic necessities in such manner as, in their minds, to warrant the conclusions herein stated.

The Committee has not considered it within its province to make exact engineering considerations, plans, and specification of method—such work being rather within the province of the Public Service Commission, who with due authority could provide the necessary departmental facilities for determination of the method of practical execution of the general plan here recommended.

Nor does the Committee consider it within its scope to deal with the strictly commercial problem of costs and revenues following upon such a plan, for the reason that the costs will depend in large degree upon the specific methods adopted, while the revenues must necessarily be of such long continuing character through many years as to reach into traffic problems beyond present vision.

CONTROLLING ELEMENTS.

THE following statements are believed by the Committee to underlie and largely control the determination of this problem.

West Street is 70 feet wide and extends from Battery Park to West 60th Street.

The City owns for nearly all this distance a Marginal Way 180 feet wide, between West Street and the Bulkhead Line. This marginal way has cost the City approximately $40,000,000. It is available for any purpose to which the City chooses to put it, and has been acquired primarily to facilitate the handling of ocean, coastwise, and rail freight.

There is ample evidence on record, not necessary to incorporate here, to indicate that the great bulk of water front freight can be most cheaply and conveniently handled, from point to point around the entire harbor frontage, on the water—by floats, lighters, and otherwise,—and that a marginal railroad as the principal freight facility along a water front such as the Hudson River is inadequate, impractical, and undesirable.

It is, however, believed to be equally true that limited rail freight handling facilities along such water front will be found useful and economical and that this use and economy would increase with time

It is also obvious that such freight traffic facilities must be upon some form of viaduct structure—provided with adequate means for elevating and lowering freight between floats and structures (or the equivalent) and with such connection to warehouses and piers as may appear most suitable in the development of the design.

Provisions should be made from time to time for warehouses along the water front, so related to the steamship piers and viaduct railway as to enable such interchange of freight to be made as may hereafter, through growth, be found necessary without the present double haul cartage to and from warehouses many blocks inland. Such warehouses can perhaps be best located on the marginal way owned by the City, with first floors at such height as to leave clear way for truckage beneath, and so related by handling facilities to piers and existing railway freight termini as to facilitate the interchange of freight between warehouses and piers and the handling of cars and freight from the street or float level to the viaduct, for distribution.

The surface horse car line on West Street needs to be removed to make this street a clear way for trucking. It should be replaced with a passenger viaduct structure,—which would obviously be an integral part of the freight viaduct,—for handling with electrical equipment the existing West Street passenger traffic and its reasonable future increase. Provision should also be made for such additional passenger service as may be brought to this line through other traffic connections hereafter referred to. Two tracks might suffice, while under certain possible conditions it may evolve into a three or four-track passenger railway,—for which development due allowance should be made.

The fact that footings for either viaducts or warehouses would be difficult and expensive along this water front is duly apprehended, but that such footings can be obtained is not so much a matter of doubt as of cost, and what constitutes warranted cost at one time may differ widely from warranted cost at another.

ADDITIONAL PASSENGER TRANSPORTATION.

ADDITIONAL passenger transportation is needed on the West Side of Manhattan Island and the proposed West Street Development affords a simple and comparatively inexpensive solution of this ever-increasing necessity. This would be accomplished by an extension of the West Street passenger viaduct facilities through Tenth Avenue into Amsterdam Avenue, and at some proper point descending to a subway, thence to a terminus at Fort George, which is the most direct and rapid route through New York City.

REMOVAL OF SURFACE TRACKS.

AN important feature of this West Side Problem is the N. Y. C. & H. R. R. R. freight track readjustment, in connection with which it is obvious that it is to the interest of the City, the West Side property owners, the public generally, and to the Railroad to have the tracks removed from the surface of the streets between the 60th Street Yards and St. Johns Park.

It is the belief of your Committee that any plan of effecting this mainly through the construction of subways to accommodate standard railway equipment is undesirable, uncommercial, and operatively impractical. It is also the belief of the Committee that an elevated structure for this purpose, following or approximating the present route, would be undesirable when built and eventually intolerable.

UNDERGROUND FREIGHT TRACKS EMERGING TO OVERHEAD FREIGHT TRACKS.

THE N. Y. C. & H. R. R. R. Co. has heretofore indicated its willingness to construct a freight subway from its 60th Street Yards to about 30th Street, emerging to such elevated structure as may be approved leading thence to St. Johns Park Freight Yards. This plan would require proper provision for connection with the 30th Street Freight Yards and have due regard to the necessity of an over-crossing of the Ninth Avenue Elevated Road.

Inspection indicates several embarrassments to this plan—chief among which is the objectionable occupation of City streets in making the emergence from such a subway, requiring nearly 5,000 feet of reasonable gradient. This means that practically one mile of street would be used in such a manner that on about one-half of it traffic would be unable to cross over it and on the remaining half-mile would be unable to cross under it, thus practically closing the street for traffic crossing the same to this large extent.

ELEVATED FREIGHT TRACKS.

A MORE consistent and practical method, in the opinion of your Committee, is to continue the proposed marginal freight viaduct from Gansevoort Street along the Marginal Way to about West 59th Street, then swinging into the 60th Street Yards, with spurs at about West 33d Street leading to the 30th Street and intermediate yards.

In view of the foregoing and various studies by the Committee of alternate arrangements, the Committee recommends the following:

RECOMMENDATIONS.

I. The City to construct on West Street and such part of the Marginal Way as may be necessary a Freight Railway Viaduct of two tracks capacity, or a Freight and Passenger Railway Viaduct of four tracks, from a point at or near Battery Place to the freight yards of the N. Y. C. & H. R. R. R. at 59th Street. This viaduct to follow the route of West Street for its whole length.

If for freight purposes only, to connect with the local freight house at St. Johns Park, or its equivalent, and the freight yards of the Railroad near 33d Street, and to be arranged to serve tracks in the second floors of wharf or warehouse buildings as may be necessary from time to time in the future.

If for both freight and passenger purposes, two of the four tracks to serve as a passenger train route in connection with railroad tracks from 59th Street to Spuyten Duyvil and beyond, and also, if desired, by an underground cross-connection with the Putnam Division of the N. Y. C. & H. R. R. R. at or near 155th Street.

This viaduct to be used by the N. Y. C. & H. R. R. R. under proper agreement with the City, and the N. Y. C. & H. R. R. R. tracks on the surface of all streets southerly of 60th Street Freight Yards to be removed.

This freight viaduct also to be used, under proper agreements with the City, by the several railroads approaching the City from the West and South when and so far as such use shall be found desirable or best for the public welfare. A study to be made of the existing trackage and yards of such railroads on Manhattan Island with a view to providing practical means of future replacement of existing facilities through this marginal freight viaduct, and marginal warehouses.

II. The City to arrange the above viaduct south of Gansevoort Street so that it may construct as soon as practicable either an additional two or four-track Manhattan Island Rapid Transit Express or Local Passenger Railroad from Battery Place to Fort George via West Street, Tenth Avenue, and Amsterdam Avenue. This railroad to be a viaduct structure from Battery Place to about 59th Street and a subway structure (except at Manhattan Valley) for the remainder of the distance. The grades of the viaduct portion to be arranged so as not to interfere with necessary spur tracks for freight viaduct crossings to a down-town freight house near Canal Street or spur tracks to other warehouses, or with foot bridges over West Street leading to the ferries.

These grades should be arranged so that foot bridges may be constructed over the street from the east side of West Street to the passenger ferry stations at various points and at the same time have the foot bridges under the elevated structures. The grades on the elevated structures for rapid transit purposes should be arranged so that spurs from the elevated freight structure could be turned easterly at various points and cross under the passenger structure.

The horse car tracks on the surface of West Street to be removed when the passenger viaduct is erected.

III. Warehouses to be constructed along the river front, either on the marginal way or near by, from time to time as demanded by the growth and character of commerce, to the end that trucking to and from warehouses remote from the river front may be reduced to a minimum.

These warehouses when constructed to be served by spurs from the main freight tracks in West Street; also to be connected to the piers by means of auxiliary conveyances for handling either car borne or water borne traffic.

DIVISION OF SPACE IN MARGINAL WAY.

FOUR rapid transit passenger tracks and four others for freight and suburban passenger service would occupy about 100 feet in width, except at stations. As West Street is 70 feet wide and its Marginal Way 180 feet wide, there is left 150 feet available for clearance over easterly sidewalk of West Street and warehouses near docks. Allowing 20 feet for the sidewalk clearance, there remains 130 feet for warehouses, which includes the 50 feet on which bulkhead freight sheds have been permitted to a limited extent.

RIVERSIDE PARK IMPROVEMENT.

YOUR Committee is aware of negotiations which have heretofore been held between the City and the N. Y. C. & H. R. R. R. Co. for additional tracks along the river front above 60th Street in consideration of the Company assuming the expense of covering its tracks with a deck which shall be provided in the form of a plaza extension of Riverside Park.

In view of this, your Committee would suggest that in event of these additional tracks being thus placed in connection with the park improvement above referred to, it might be found especially advantageous to the rapid transit facilities of the City to provide for a certain amount of suburban passenger service down these tracks and over the West Side Viaduct, as mentioned in the third paragraph of "I," thus relieving the congestion in the Park Avenue Tunnel,—thereby conducing to public safety and also relieving pressure on the Subway below 42d Street.

THE PUTNAM BRANCH.

THE Putnam Branch of the N. Y. C. & H. R. R. R. could, as previously indicated, turn westward at about 155th Street and by subway connect with the waterside tracks; or it could connect with the proposed Amsterdam Avenue subway—thus in either case relieving congestion of rapid transit facilities of the upper West Side.

It is also possible, if found desirable, to turn the proposed passenger traffic of the waterside tracks eastward at about 155th Street and thence down the Amsterdam Avenue Subway to the West Street Marginal Way at Gansevoort Street.

CONNECTION WITH GRAND CENTRAL STATION.

IT is also suggested that all of the above would be consistent with the plan heretofore made public of turning certain N. Y. C. & H. R. R. R. tracks westward from Park Avenue north of 53d Street, making a subway connection with the West Side tracks to relieve congestion in the Park Avenue Tunnel.

PRESERVING THE EQUIVALENT OF PRESENT FACILITIES.

YOUR Committee recognizes the importance, both to the N. Y. C. & H. R. R. R. and to the City, of preserving freight facilities equal to those now existing and foresees that it may be necessary, in the process of vacating existing rights, to afford the Railroad Company in return substantially equal freight facilities, and if in conjunction therewith the City can induce the Railroad Company to provide certain West Side passenger facilities, a public benefit will result with no offsetting detriment. Such passenger traffic should eventually be sufficiently remunerative to warrant the Railroad Company in assenting to the proposed change.

PASSENGER TERMINAL NECESSITIES ALONG WEST STREET.

IN order to emphasize the desirability of so locating freight tracks in West Street southerly of Gansevoort Street that they may not interfere with a West Street rapid transit passenger route, attention is called to the enormous passenger traffic which comes to or departs from New York, along this street, independently of the fact that a rapid transit route from the upper end of Manhattan Island would deliver or take a great number of people from the congested district of the City below Canal Street in quicker time than any other route. This street is at present the locality for the terminal site of all railroads which reach New York from the South and West (excepting the N. Y. C. & H. R. R. R.) and the terminal site of nearly all the ocean steamship passenger traffic, as well as the Hudson River, Long Island Sound, and near-by shore excursion boats. These terminal sites give to West Street a greater point of centralization for passengers than is generally apprehended.

IMMEDIATE RESULTS.

IT has been the object of your Committee to devise some plan which shall produce betterment to all concerned, and it is its belief that if a plan substantially as above outlined can be perfected it will immediately result in a better condition in every respect, and will afford an opportunity, on a scale commensurate with the increasing density of this insular metropolis, for future growth of West Side freight and passenger traffic which will eventually be of great benefit to the City and to the West Side property owners.

The plan, as here outlined, does not involve the construction of extensive warehouse properties in the first instance, nor is it essential that they should ever be constructed for the carrying out of the main transportation considerations. All plans, however, should comprehend and provide for the opportunity for this extensive marginal warehouse plan, in order that its possible future advantages may be embraced.

It should be noted that if the recommendations of your Committee are adopted they provide for the carrying out of these improvements step by step, and permit of obtaining the benefits of each step without necessarily executing the balance,—each step being complete in itself.

The result of the first step would be the removal of all N. Y. C. & H. R. R. R. tracks now existing on the surface of the streets.

The result of another step would be provision for increased rapid transit for passengers on the West Side of the City, which would be superior in speed to any rapid transit provision now existing which moves passengers from the upper end of Manhattan Island to down town points, and the elimination of the Belt Line surface tracks now on West Street.

The remaining step provides for the construction of warehouses on the westerly side of the Marginal Way and adjacent to the piers, in which merchandise may be stored without its being carted through the streets to storage warehouses remote from the water front, thus materially relieving the streets from team congestion.

MOTIVE POWER.

IN considering the question of improvement of railroad facilities, it has been assumed that the motive power for handling all trains upon all tracks shall eventually be electric, and that steam locomotives shall be abandoned on Manhattan Island except for emergency service.

NON-INTERFERENCE WITH FUTURE DEVELOPMENTS.

THIS problem of West Side transportation can be extended almost indefinitely with reference to freight and passenger traffic to include many plans and facilities, but this Committee has not thought it expedient to thus complicate the problem with the many possibilities of the future; but rather to attempt to discern a comparatively simple development which will meet certain present needs and be elastically adaptable to future developments.

Viewed in this light, it is believed:

That, whatever be the development of urban freight handling, there will be found need of as much warehouse room as the marginal way will reasonably accommodate;

That, whatever be developed by way of subway system of freight distribution, there will be found need of as many tracks as can consistently be placed on a West Street viaduct;

That such tracks represent a transportation facility that can without material modification be utilized for freight or passenger service, as the necessities of any given time require;

That the early construction of a plan based on these recommendations will begin a process of relief, the results of which will usefully guide the development of further facilities over greater areas; and

That the plan proposed will give the earliest possible relief from surface steam freight traffic and in a manner which through minimum expense gives greatest commercial warrant, yet permitting any more expensive method to be a future consideration at such time as subway or any other method may be warranted.

CONCLUSION.

IN conclusion, your Committee recommend that this report, when laid before the Public Service Commission, be accompanied by the request that the Commission through its engineering staff make suitable plans and determinations of the method here outlined of solving the West Side Transportation Problem, together with the necessary estimates, in order that its merits may be fully developed.

Respectfully submitted,

WALTER C. KERR, *Chairman;*
WM. J. MATHESON,
E. H. OUTERBRIDGE,
GEORGE C. SMITH,
JOHN M. CARRERE,
Committee on West Side R. R. Tracks.

www.ingramcontent.com/pod-product-compliance
Lightning Source LLC
LaVergne TN
LVHW020631110826
845149LV00004B/1145
* 9 7 8 1 4 1 8 1 8 6 6 7 8 *